Milly, Molly & Runaway Bean

"We may look different but we feel the same."

Milly and Molly watched Aunt Maude plant her climbing beans. She had one left over.

"Plant this in a sunny place and you will grow fit and healthy on your very own fresh, green beans. And don't forget to water it," she snipped.

Farmer Hegarty gave Milly and Molly a bag of his special sheep manure.
"Feed this to your bean and it will grow strong and healthy," he said.

Milly and Molly fed and watered their bean every night.

The bean began to climb.

It climbed up over the wall and into the lemon tree next door.

It climbed over the fence and into the peach tree in the garden next door to that.

Milly and Molly ran to find Aunt Maude. "Our bean won't stop climbing," they said.

Aunt Maude rubbed her chin. "That bean knows exactly where it's going," she snipped. "It will stop when it gets there."

The bean climbed over a potting shed and through a hedge.

A crowd was beginning to gather. Milly and Molly's bean was famous.
"Where is it going?" they asked Aunt Maude.

"It knows exactly where it's going," snipped Aunt Maude. "It will stop when it gets there."

The bean climbed up a drainpipe and in through a window.

Lying in bed beneath the window was a very unwell little boy.

"I'm going to give you fresh, green beans to make you fit and healthy," whispered the bean.

The unwell little boy couldn't believe the famous bean had come specially to see him. "Thank you," he said weakly.

The bean stopped climbing. Word got about that it was giving fresh, green beans to an unwell little boy.

"What did I tell you," snipped Aunt Maude. "That bean knew exactly where it was going."

The unwell little boy ate the fresh, green beans and grew stronger and stronger.

Then one morning, he opened his front door and walked out into the sunshine. An almighty cheer went up from the crowd.

"There," snipped Aunt Maude. "Our fresh, green beans made you grow fit and healthy."

"I'm sure my bag of special sheep manure had something to do with it," mused Farmer Hegarty.

"Fiddlesticks," snipped Aunt Maude. "That bean knew exactly where it was going."